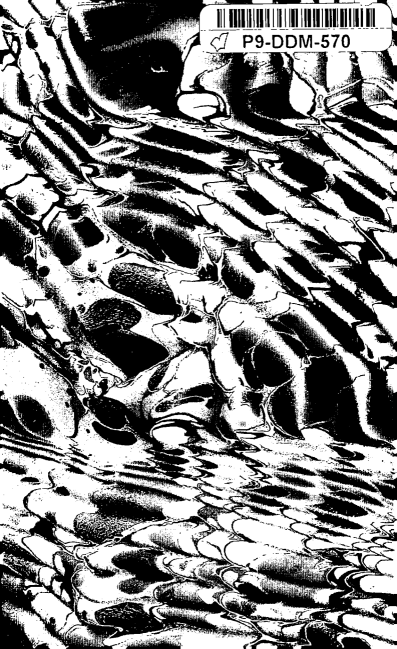

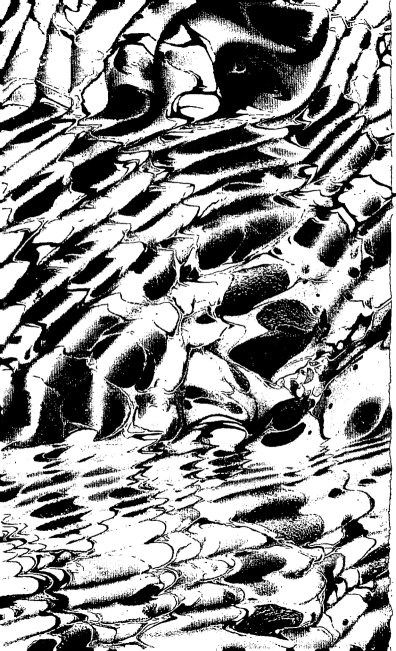

The Spirit of America

To _____

From _____

Also by Barbara Milo Ohrbach

The Scented Room

The Scented Room
Gardening Notebook

Antiques at Home

A Token of Friendship

Memories of Childhood

A Bouquet of Flowers

A Cheerful Heart

BY

BARBARA MILO OHRBACH

★ ·★ ★ ☆ ★

*A Collection of Favorite American
Quotes, Poems, Songs, and Recipes*

 CLARKSON POTTER/PUBLISHERS
NEW YORK

Grateful acknowledgment is made to the following for permission to reprint
previously published material: "Western Star" by Stephen Vincent Benét,
reprinted by permission of Brandt & Brandt, Literary Agents, Inc.

Every effort has been made to locate the copyright holders of materials used in
this book. Should there be any omissions or errors, we apologize and shall be
pleased to make the appropriate acknowledgments in future editions.

Published by Clarkson N. Potter, Inc., 201 East 50th Street,
New York, New York 10022. Member of the Crown Publishing Group.

CLARKSON N. POTTER, POTTER, and colophon are trademarks of
. Clarkson N. Potter, Inc.

Manufactured in Japan

Design by Justine Strasberg

Library of Congress Cataloging-in-Publication Data
The Spirit of America: a collection of favorite American quotes, poems, songs,
and recipes/[compiled] by Barbara Milo Ohrbach.—1st ed.
1. Patriotism—United States—Quotations, maxims, etc.   2. Patriotism—
United States—Poetry.   3. Cookery, American.   4. Quotations, American.
5. American poetry.   I. Ohrbach, Barbara Milo.
E169.1.S745   1992
973—dc20   91-16419
                                                                              CIP

ISBN 0-517-58627-4
1 3 5 7 9 10 8 6 4 2
First Edition

Table of Contents

Three cheers and a big thank you to everyone whose busy, competent hands have paraded through this book: Beth Allen, Gayle Benderoff, Andrea Connolly, Martina D'Alton, Lisa Fresne, Deborah Geltman, Bill Nave, Teresa Nicholas, Mel Ohrbach, Camille Prehatney, Gloria Schaaf, Rita and Harry Singer, Carol Southern, Tina Strasberg, and Jane Treuhaft. And special thanks to my editor, Shirley Wohl.

Introduction

The American people never carry an umbrella. They prepare to walk in eternal sunshine.

ALFRED E. SMITH

These optimistic words were brought to mind recently as we stood watching our small town's annual Memorial Day celebration. They seemed so appropriate. Main Street was lined with children, parents, grandparents—all the

★　　★　　★　　★　　★　　★　　★　　★

generations together in the warm May sun.
As our neighbors in the Volunteer Fire
Department and Rescue Squad, Women's
Auxiliary, and Girl and Boy Scouts marched
past with flags flying, we all clapped and waved.
And I knew that if you visited any typical
American town you probably would find this
same sense of community spirit and pride.

We all do share a uniquely American spirit
that goes back to the very beginning, a spirit
that I hope you will find reflected here. I found
that writing this book on the five hundredth
anniversary of Columbus's discovery of America
was for me a moving journey of rediscovery, of
encountering things I hadn't read since I was in
school: the words to some of our most beloved
national songs, familiar documents such as the
Declaration of Independence, and the thoughts
of many of those who helped to shape this
extraordinary country, from Thomas Jefferson,
Abraham Lincoln, Thomas Paine, and Susan
B. Anthony to Daniel Webster, Frederick
Douglass, Clara Barton, and Oliver Wendell
Holmes. Their intelligence and fairness, together with common sense and simple faith in
the Golden Rule, are today a lesson for us all.

As I worked on this book, I recalled the
unity of spirit I sensed at that Memorial Day
parade. Isn't it time we all made this pulling
together an everyday thing? Listen to the words
of Edward Everett Hale—

★　　★　　★　　★　　★　　★　　★　　★

★ ★ ★ ★ ★ ★ ★ ★

To look up and not down,
To look forward and not back,
To look out and not in, and
To lend a hand.

We can still make a difference in the lives of others. As my mother used to say, rolling up her sleeves, there are some things you "have to do yourself." Volunteer, help someone learn to read, plant a tree, keep an eye on an elderly neighbor, become a Big Brother or Sister, support education, stop the destruction of our public lands, do more for the young and the poor—and above all, *set an example.* It's time to stop feeling that we can't change things—time to get involved by expressing our concern to our representatives, by making ourselves heard loud and clear. Let's get back to basics, the sturdy American values, the lasting values that we in this country hold dear.

Barbara Milo Ohrbach
New York

★ ★ ★ ★ ★ ★ ★ ★

My God! how little do my countrymen know what precious blessings they are in possession of, and which no other people on earth enjoy!

THOMAS JEFFERSON

The things that will destroy America are prosperity at any price, peace at any price, safety first instead of duty first, the love of soft living, and the get-rich-quick theory of life. This country will not be a permanently good place for us to live unless it's a good place for all of us to live.

THEODORE ROOSEVELT

There are those, I know, who will say that the liberation of humanity, the freedom of man and mind, is nothing but a dream. They are right. It is. It is the American dream.

ARCHIBALD MACLEISH

1

"Still, whatever fate betide us children of the flag are we!"

Brown Cow Ice Cream Soda

*A*fter school, I could always find my pals at the soda fountain in town. Thornton Wilder's ". . . enjoy your ice-cream while it's on your plate, that's my philosophy" seemed like good advice then, and it still is.

¼ CUP CHOCOLATE SYRUP

3 SCOOPS VANILLA ICE CREAM

CHILLED ROOT BEER

1 LARGE SPOONFUL WHIPPED CREAM

★ Pour the syrup into a tall soda glass, add 1 scoop of the ice cream, and stir until smooth.
★ Pour a steady stream of root beer slowly into the glass until it is half-full.
★ Add the remaining 2 scoops of ice cream, then finish filling the glass with root beer.
★ Top with the whipped cream.
★ To make a black-and-white soda, use 2 scoops of vanilla ice cream and 1 scoop of chocolate. Substitute seltzer for the root beer.
★ To make a Stars-and-Stripes soda, use strawberry syrup instead of chocolate, and 2 scoops of strawberry ice cream and 1 scoop of vanilla. Substitute seltzer for the root beer.

MAKES 1 ICE CREAM SODA

The United States is the only country with a known birthday.

JAMES G. BLAINE

America has quite rightly been called a nation that was "born free."

J. W. FULBRIGHT

Sometimes people call me an idealist. Well, that is the way I know I am an American. America is the only idealistic nation in the world.

WOODROW WILSON

 America is a willingness of the heart.

F. SCOTT FITZGERALD

★

And so, my fellow Americans: ask not what your country can do for you—ask what you can do for your country.

JOHN F. KENNEDY

God pity the American citizen who does not love the flag.

BENJAMIN HARRISON

I hear America singing, the varied carols I hear.

WALT WHITMAN

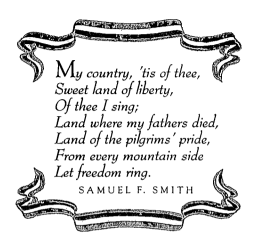

My country, 'tis of thee,
Sweet land of liberty,
Of thee I sing;
Land where my fathers died,
Land of the pilgrims' pride,
From every mountain side
Let freedom ring.

SAMUEL F. SMITH

America is a tune. It must be sung together.

GERARD STANLEY LEE

O beautiful for spacious skies,
For amber waves of grain,
For purple mountain majesties
Above the fruited plain!
America! America!
God shed His grace on thee,
And crown thy good with brotherhood
From sea to shining sea!

KATHARINE LEE BATES

5

Thanksgiving Joys

Mom's Old-Fashioned Apple Pie

Nothing's more American than apple pie, perhaps because we grow some of the tastiest apples here. Try Jonathans, Granny Smiths, Northern Spy, Baldwins, or Winesaps in this favorite recipe, and serve warm.

3 POUNDS BAKING APPLES

2 TABLESPOONS LEMON JUICE

1 CUP SUGAR

2 TABLESPOONS FLOUR

2 TABLESPOONS CINNAMON

½ TEASPOON SALT

1 FROZEN DEEP-DISH 9-INCH, 2-CRUST PIE SHELL

2 TABLESPOONS BUTTER

1 EGG

1 TABLESPOON WATER

★ Preheat oven to 425°F.

★ Peel, core, and thinly slice the apples into a bowl, then toss with the lemon juice.

★ In a bowl, mix the sugar, flour, cinnamon, and salt, then toss with the apples.

★ Mound the apples on the bottom pie crust and dot with the butter.

★ Form the top crust, per package directions.

★ In a bowl, beat the egg with the water, then brush generously on the top crust.

★ Bake for 10 minutes, reduce heat to 350°F., and bake 50 minutes, until golden brown.

MAKES 1 PIE OR 8 SERVINGS

We must learn to live together as brothers or
perish together as fools.

MARTIN LUTHER KING, JR.

Peace, like charity, begins at home.

FRANKLIN D. ROOSEVELT

Let us have peace.

ULYSSES S. GRANT

There never was a good war or a bad peace.

BENJAMIN FRANKLIN

★

I cannot raise my hand against my
birthplace, my home, my children. I should like,
above all things, that our difficulties might be
peaceably arranged . . .

ROBERT E. LEE

8

I esteem it a chief felicity of this country that it excels in women.

RALPH WALDO EMERSON

Without the United Nations our country would walk alone, ruled by fear, instead of confidence and hope.

ELEANOR ROOSEVELT

While our soldiers stand and fight, I can stand and feed and nurse them.

CLARA BARTON

In the new code of laws . . . I desire you would remember the ladies and be more generous and favorable to them than your ancestors.

ABIGAIL ADAMS

Abraham Lincoln said: "No man is good enough to govern another man without his consent." Now I say unto you, "No man is good enough to govern any woman without her consent."

SUSAN B. ANTHONY

State Flowers

ALABAMA . . . . *Camellia*
ALASKA . . . . *Forget-me-not*
ARIZONA. . . . . . *Saguaro Cactus Blossom*
ARKANSAS . . . . *Apple Blossom*
CALIFORNIA . . . . . . *Golden Poppy*
COLORADO . . . . *Columbine*
CONNECTICUT . . . . *Mountain Laurel*
DELAWARE . . . . *Peach Blossom*
FLORIDA . . . . *Orange Blossom*
GEORGIA. . . . . *Cherokee Rose*
HAWAII. . . . . *Hibiscus*
IDAHO. . . . . *Syringa*
ILLINOIS . . . . *Meadow Violet*
INDIANA . . . . *Peony*
IOWA . . . . *Wild Rose*
KANSAS . . . . *Sunflower*
KENTUCKY . . . . *Goldenrod*
LOUISIANA . . . . *Magnolia Blossom*
MAINE. . . . . *Pinecone and Tassel*
MARYLAND . . . . *Black-eyed Susan*
MASSACHUSETTS . . *Mayflower*
MICHIGAN . . . . *Apple Blossom*
MINNESOTA . . . . . . *Lady's-slipper*

State	Flower
MISSISSIPPI	*Magnolia*
MISSOURI	*Hawthorn*
MONTANA	*Bitterroot*
NEBRASKA	*Goldenrod*
NEVADA	*Sagebrush*
NEW HAMPSHIRE	*Purple Lilac*
NEW JERSEY	*Purple Violet*
NEW MEXICO	*Yucca*
NEW YORK	*Rose*
NORTH CAROLINA	*Dogwood*
NORTH DAKOTA	*Wild Prairie Rose*
OHIO	*Red Carnation*
OKLAHOMA	*Mistletoe*
OREGON	*Oregon Grape*
PENNSYLVANIA	*Mountain Laurel*
RHODE ISLAND	*Violet*
SOUTH CAROLINA	*Carolina Jessamine*
SOUTH DAKOTA	*American Pasque*
TENNESSEE	*Iris*
TEXAS	*Bluebonnet*
UTAH	*Sego Lily*
VERMONT	*Red Clover*
VIRGINIA	*American Dogwood*
WASHINGTON	*Rhododendron*
WEST VIRGINIA	*Rhododendron*
WISCONSIN	*Butterfly Violet*
WYOMING	*Indian Paintbrush*

I *am not a Virginian, but an American.*

T*o love freedom is a tendency that many Americans are born with.*

E. B. WHITE

★

A*t the bottom of all the tributes paid to democracy is the little man, walking into the little booth, with a little pencil, making a little cross on a little bit of paper.*

WINSTON CHURCHILL

S*uperman, disguised as Clark Kent, mild-mannered reporter for a great metropolitan newspaper, fights a never-ending battle for truth, justice, and the American way.*

INTRODUCTION TO RADIO SERIES

I*f a man is going to be an American at all let him be so without any qualifying adjectives; and if he is going to be something else, let him drop the word American from his personal description.*

HENRY CABOT LODGE

Ours is the only country deliberately founded on a good idea.

JOHN GUNTHER

I was born an American; I live an American; I shall die an American.

DANIEL WEBSTER

The American Nation! Its men are as brave, energetic and dauntless as they are honest.

NICHOLAS, CZAR OF RUSSIA

I don't make jokes—I just watch the government and report the facts.

WILL ROGERS

The fabulous country—the place where miracles not only happen, but where they happen all the time.

THOMAS WOLFE

W... ...no glory but his co...

All-American Macaroni and Cheese

"*Yankee Doodle came to town riding on a pony; Stuck a feather in his cap and called it Macaroni.*" Doesn't this bring back memories of lunch in your old school cafeteria?

½ POUND ELBOW MACARONI
¼ CUP BUTTER
¼ CUP MINCED ONION
¼ CUP FLOUR
½ TEASPOON NUTMEG
½ TEASPOON SALT

1½ CUPS MILK
1 TABLESPOON WORCESTERSHIRE
⅛ TEASPOON CAYENNE PEPPER
¼ POUND SHARP CHEDDAR CHEESE

★ Preheat oven to 350°F. Butter a shallow 12-inch round baking dish.

★ Cook macaroni until tender. Drain and place in baking dish.

★ Melt the butter in a saucepan, add the onion, and cook until translucent.

★ Stir in flour, nutmeg, and salt, and cook for 1 minute. Slowly stir in milk, Worcestershire, and pepper, and continue cooking until slightly thick. Remove from the heat.

★ Stir in the cheese until it melts, then pour over the macaroni.

★ Bake for 25 minutes, until browned.

MAKES 4 SERVINGS

Father, I cannot tell a lie, I did it with my little hatchet.

GEORGE WASHINGTON

I am not surprised at what George has done, for he was always a good boy.

MARY WASHINGTON, HIS MOTHER

The filial love of Washington for his mother is an attribute of American manhood, a badge which invites our trust and confidence and an indispensable element of American greatness.

GROVER CLEVELAND

I hope I shall always possess firmness and virtue enough to maintain what I consider the most enviable of all titles, the character of an "Honest Man."

GEORGE WASHINGTON

One of the greatest captains of the age.

BENJAMIN FRANKLIN

First Citizen of Earth.

JAMES J. ROCHE

Oh, Washington! thou hero, patriot, sage,
Friend of all climes and pride of every age!

THOMAS PAINE

Put none but Americans on guard to-night.

GEORGE WASHINGTON

He was great as he was good; he was great
because he was good.

EDWARD EVERETT

First in war, first in peace, first in the hearts of
his countrymen.

HENRY LEE

Liberty, when it begins to take root, is a plant of
rapid growth.

GEORGE WASHINGTON

4TH JULY GREETINGS

Homemade Back Porch Lemonade

H*arry S. Truman was known for his homespun wisdom, such as "If you can't stand the heat, get out of the kitchen." I couldn't agree more. On hot summer days all I want to do is sit outdoors, sipping homemade lemonade and listening to the birds.*

15 LARGE LEMONS
3 CUPS SUGAR
2 CUPS WATER

ICE CUBES
2 CUPS COLD WATER
FRESH MINT

★ Thinly slice 2 of the lemons and set aside.
★ Slice a third lemon and place in a saucepan with the sugar and water. Bring to a boil over high heat until the sugar dissolves, then boil for 10 more minutes. Remove from heat.
★ Squeeze the 12 remaining lemons to make 2 cups of juice. Stir into the sugar syrup, then strain the mixture into a pitcher.
★ Add 20 ice cubes plus the cold water and the reserved lemon slices, then chill.
★ To serve, stir in 20 additional ice cubes and 5 sprigs of mint.
★ Fill tall glasses with ice, pour in lemonade, and garnish each with a fresh mint leaf.

MAKES 2 QUARTS OR 8 SERVINGS

The United States is the best and fairest and most decent nation on the face of the earth.

GEORGE BUSH

A nation reveals itself not only by the men it produces but also by the men it honors, the men it remembers.

JOHN F. KENNEDY

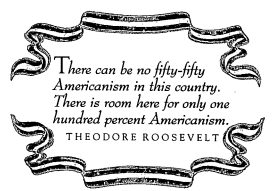

There can be no fifty-fifty Americanism in this country. There is room here for only one hundred percent Americanism.

THEODORE ROOSEVELT

The American system of rugged individualism.

HERBERT CLARK HOOVER

Whatever America hopes to bring to pass in this world must first come to pass in the heart of America.

DWIGHT D. EISENHOWER

The buck stops here.

HARRY S. TRUMAN

Nobody can acquire honor by doing what is wrong.

THOMAS JEFFERSON

Sir, I would rather be right than President.

HENRY CLAY

One man with courage makes a majority.

ANDREW JACKSON

The world must be made safe for democracy.

WOODROW WILSON

*National honor is national property of the
highest value.*

JAMES MONROE

State Birds

ALABAMA	*Yellowhammer*
ALASKA	*Yellow Ptarmigan*
ARIZONA	*Cactus Wren*
ARKANSAS	*Mockingbird*
CALIFORNIA	*Valley Quail*
COLORADO	*Lark Bunting*
CONNECTICUT	*American Robin*
DELAWARE	*Blue Hen Chicken*
FLORIDA	*Mockingbird*
GEORGIA	*Brown Thrasher*
HAWAII	*Nene*
IDAHO	*Mountain Bluebird*
ILLINOIS	*Eastern Cardinal*
INDIANA	*Cardinal*
IOWA	*Goldfinch*
KANSAS	*Western Meadowlark*
KENTUCKY	*Kentucky Cardinal*
LOUISIANA	*Brown Pelican*
MAINE	*Chickadee*
MARYLAND	*Baltimore Oriole*
MASSACHUSETTS	*Chickadee*
MICHIGAN	*Robin*
MINNESOTA	*Common Loon*

MISSISSIPPI	*Mockingbird*
MISSOURI	*Eastern Bluebird*
MONTANA	*Western Meadowlark*
NEBRASKA	*Western Meadowlark*
NEVADA	*Mountain Bluebird*
NEW HAMPSHIRE	*Purple Finch*
NEW JERSEY	*Eastern Goldfinch*
NEW MEXICO	*Roadrunner*
NEW YORK	*Bluebird*
NORTH CAROLINA	*Cardinal*
NORTH DAKOTA	*Meadowlark*
OHIO	*Cardinal*
OKLAHOMA	*Scissortailed Flycatcher*
OREGON	*Western Meadowlark*
PENNSYLVANIA	*Ruffed Grouse*
RHODE ISLAND	*Rhode Island Red*
SOUTH CAROLINA	*Carolina Wren*
SOUTH DAKOTA	*Ring-necked Pheasant*
TENNESSEE	*Mockingbird*
TEXAS	*Mockingbird*
UTAH	*Sea Gull*
VERMONT	*Hermit Thrush*
VIRGINIA	*Cardinal*
WASHINGTON	*Willow Goldfinch*
WEST VIRGINIA	*Cardinal*
WISCONSIN	*Robin*
WYOMING	*Western Meadowlark*

Hats off!
Along the streets there comes
A blare of bugles, a ruffle of drums,
A flash of colour beneath the sky:
  Hats off!
 The flag is passing by!

HENRY HOLCOMB BENNETT

Oh, it may be a scoundrel's flag, too, and a
drummer's flag, and a fraud's flag, and a thief's
flag. But first and foremost, it is a man's flag.

RUSSELL BAKER

On my honor, I will try:
To serve God and my country,
To help people at all times,
And to live by the Girl Scout Law.

THE GIRL SCOUT PLEDGE

On my honor I will do my best—
  To do my duty to God and my country, and to
  obey the scout law;
  To help other people at all times;
  To keep myself physically strong, mentally
  awake, and morally straight.

THE BOY SCOUT OATH

24

You're a Grand Old Flag.

GEORGE M. COHAN

Oh! say, can you see, by the dawn's early light,
What so proudly we hailed at the twilight's last
     gleaming?
Whose broad stripes and bright stars, thro' the
     perilous fight,
O'er the ramparts we watched were so gallantly
     streaming?
And the rockets' red glare, the bombs bursting
     in air,
Gave proof thro' the night that our flag was still
     there.
Oh! say, does that star-spangled banner yet
     wave
O'er the land of the free and the home of the
     brave?

FRANCIS SCOTT KEY

Up rose old Barbara Frietchie then,
Bowed with her fourscore years and ten,
"Shoot, if you must, this old gray head,
But spare your country's flag," she said.

JOHN GREENLEAF WHITTIER

One flag, one land, one heart, one hand,
One nation, evermore!

OLIVER WENDELL HOLMES

25

Oh, where treads the foot that would falter for thee

Crunchy Fried Chicken

E*ach of my southern friends has a favorite family recipe for fried chicken. This one is generations old, very crunchy, and very, very good.*

6 POUNDS CHICKEN PIECES	3 CUPS FLOUR
3 TABLESPOONS SEASONED SALT	2 TABLESPOONS PAPRIKA
	2 EGGS
2 TABLESPOONS THYME	3 CUPS BUTTERMILK
2 TEASPOONS BLACK PEPPER	2 CUPS VEGETABLE OIL

★ Wash the chicken pieces and dry.
★ In a bowl, mix the salt, thyme, and pepper, then rub the chicken with ½ of this mixture.
★ On a platter, mix the flour with the remaining spice mixture and the paprika.
★ In a bowl, whisk the eggs and buttermilk. Dip in the coated chicken pieces, then roll them in the flour mixture, coating well.
★ Heat 1 inch of the oil in a skillet over medium heat. Fry the chicken, turning once, about 45 minutes, until the crust is crisp.
★ Drain on racks in single layers to ensure the crispiest chicken possible.

MAKES 8 SERVINGS

What a glorious morning for America!

SAMUEL ADAMS

United we stand, divided we fall.

ANONYMOUS

E *Pluribus Unum. (One from many.)*

MOTTO FOR SEAL OF THE UNITED STATES

In this world nothing is certain but death and taxes.

BENJAMIN FRANKLIN

These are the times that try men's souls.

THOMAS PAINE

One country, one constitution, one destiny.

DANIEL WEBSTER

Taxation without representation is tyranny.

JAMES OTIS

Yesterday the greatest question was decided which ever was debated in America. . . . A resolution was passed without one dissenting colony, that these United Colonies are, and of right ought to be, free and independent States.

JOHN ADAMS

We hold these truths to be self-evident, that all men are created equal, that they are endowed by their Creator with certain unalienable Rights, that among these are Life, Liberty and the pursuit of Happiness.

THOMAS JEFFERSON,
DECLARATION OF INDEPENDENCE

We, the people of the United States, in order to form a more perfect Union, establish justice, insure domestic tranquility, provide for the common defense, promote the general welfare, and secure the blessings of liberty to ourselves and our posterity, do ordain and establish this Constitution for the United States of America.

CONSTITUTION OF THE UNITED STATES

I know not what course others may take; but as for me, give me liberty or give me death.

PATRICK HENRY

MEMORIAL DAY SOUVENIR

BETSY ROSS MAKING THE FIRST FLAG WITH STARS AND STRIPES.

Tangy Texas B-B-Q Sauce

When Talleyrand visited America, he said, "I found there a country with thirty-two religions and only one sauce." If this was the one, you may never need another!

½ CUP UNSALTED BUTTER
2 CUPS CHOPPED ONION
3 CLOVES MINCED GARLIC
32 OUNCES KETCHUP
1½ CUPS CIDER VINEGAR
1 CUP CHILI SAUCE
1 CUP DARK MOLASSES
1 CUP PACKED DARK BROWN SUGAR
⅓ CUP WORCESTERSHIRE
¼ CUP LIQUID SMOKE
2 TABLESPOONS DRY MUSTARD
2 TEASPOONS HOT-PEPPER SAUCE

☆ In a large saucepan, melt the butter over medium-high heat. Add the onion and garlic and cook until translucent.

☆ Remove from the heat and stir in the remaining ingredients.

☆ Bring to a boil over medium-high heat, then reduce heat and simmer 30 minutes.

☆ Process the sauce in a food processor or blender until smooth.

☆ Refrigerate or freeze any extra sauce.

MAKES 2 QUARTS SAUCE

Fourscore and seven years ago our fathers
brought forth on this continent a new nation,
conceived in liberty, and dedicated to the
proposition that all men are created equal.

ABRAHAM LINCOLN

I intend no modification of my oft-expressed
personal wish that all men everywhere could be
free.

ABRAHAM LINCOLN

You can fool some of the people all the time and
all the people some of the time; but you can't fool
all the people all the time.

ABRAHAM LINCOLN

The Lord prefers common-looking people. That
is why he makes so many of them.

ABRAHAM LINCOLN

Abraham Lincoln was the genius of common
sense.

CHARLES DUDLEY WARNER

A great man, tender of heart, strong of nerve, of boundless patience and broadest sympathy.

FREDERICK DOUGLASS

If this nation is ever destroyed, it will not be from without but from within.

ABRAHAM LINCOLN

Mine eyes have seen the glory of the coming of
    the Lord:
He is trampling out the vintage where the grapes
    of wrath are stored;
He hath loosed the fateful lightning of his terrible
    swift sword:
  His truth is marching on.
Glory! Glory! Hallelujah! Glory! Glory! Hallelujah!
Glory! Glory! Hallelujah! His truth is marching on.

JULIA WARD HOWE

I don't know who my grandfather was; I am much more concerned to know what his grandson will be.

ABRAHAM LINCOLN

"Lest we forget."

Crispy Hush Puppies

It's said that during the Civil War, soldiers tossed bits of fried batter to their hounds and whispered, "Hush, puppies," to quiet them. When you serve these with fried chicken, you won't hear a sound from around your dining table, either.

1 CUP YELLOW CORNMEAL	1 TEASPOON CRUSHED RED-PEPPER FLAKES
1 CUP FLOUR	2 EGGS
1 TABLESPOON SUGAR	¼ CUP MILK
1½ TEASPOONS BAKING POWDER	¼ CUP MINCED ONION
1 TEASPOON SALT	1 CUP VEGETABLE OIL

★ In a bowl, combine the cornmeal, flour, sugar, baking powder, salt, and pepper flakes.
★ In another bowl, whisk the eggs and milk, then stir into the cornmeal mixture, just until moistened. Add the onion.
★ In a skillet, heat 1 inch of the oil over medium-high heat, then drop in tablespoonfuls of the batter, adding oil as necessary.
★ Cook the hush puppies for 5 minutes, turning once, until golden. Drain on paper towels.

MAKES 1 DOZEN HUSH PUPPIES

Go west, young man, and grow up with the country.

HORACE GREELEY

Woodman, spare that tree!
Touch not a single bough!
In youth it sheltered me,
And I'll protect it now.

GEORGE P. MORRIS

What makes a nation in the beginning is a
good piece of geography.

ROBERT FROST

I leave this rule for others when I'm dead,
Be always sure you're right—then go ahead.

DAVY CROCKETT

Away, away, away down south in Dixie!
Away, away, away down south in Dixie!

DANIEL DECATUR EMMETT

In the United States there is more space where nobody is than where anybody is. That is what makes America what it is.

GERTRUDE STEIN

The United States themselves are essentially the greatest poem.

WALT WHITMAN

I do not own an inch of land,
But all I see is mine.

LUCY LARCOM

The frontiers are not east or west, north or south, but wherever a man fronts a fact.

HENRY DAVID THOREAU

For this is what America is all about. It is the uncrossed desert and the unclimbed ridge. It is the star that is not reached and the harvest that's sleeping in the unplowed ground.

LYNDON B. JOHNSON

State Trees

ALABAMA . . . . *Southern Pine*
ALASKA . . . . *Sitka Spruce*
ARIZONA. . . . . *Paloverde*
ARKANSAS . . . . *Shortleaf Pine*
CALIFORNIA . . . . . . *Redwood*
COLORADO . . . . *Colorado Blue Spruce*
CONNECTICUT . . . . . *White Oak*
DELAWARE . . . . *American Holly*
FLORIDA . . . . *Sabal Palm*
GEORGIA. . . . . *Live Oak*
HAWAII. . . . . *Kukui*
IDAHO. . . . . *Western White Pine*
ILLINOIS . . . . *Oak*
INDIANA. . . . . *Tulip Tree*
IOWA . . . . *Oak*
KANSAS . . . . *Cottonwood*
KENTUCKY . . . . *Tulip Poplar*
LOUISIANA . . . . . . *Bald Cypress*
MAINE. . . . . *Eastern White Pine*
MARYLAND . . . . *White Oak*
MASSACHUSETTS . . . *American Elm*
MICHIGAN . . . . *White Pine*
MINNESOTA . . . . . . *Red Pine*

MISSISSIPPI . . . . *Magnolia*
MISSOURI . . . . *Dogwood*
MONTANA . . . . *Ponderosa Pine*
NEBRASKA. . . . . *Cottonwood*
NEVADA . . . . *Single-Leaf Piñon*
NEW HAMPSHIRE. . . . . . *Paper Birch*
NEW JERSEY. . . . . *Red Oak*
NEW MEXICO. . . . . *Piñon*
NEW YORK. . . . . *Sugar Maple*
NORTH CAROLINA. . . . . *Pine*
NORTH DAKOTA . . . . . . *American Elm*
OHIO. . . . . *Ohio Buckeye*
OKLAHOMA. . . . . *Redbud*
OREGON . . . . *Douglas Fir*
PENNSYLVANIA . . . . *Eastern Hemlock*
RHODE ISLAND . . . . *Red Maple*
SOUTH CAROLINA. . . . . *Palmetto*
SOUTH DAKOTA . . . . . . *Black Hills Spruce*
TENNESSEE . . . . *Tulip Poplar*
TEXAS. . . . . *Pecan*
UTAH . . . . *Blue Spruce*
VERMONT . . . . *Sugar Maple*
VIRGINIA . . . . *American Dogwood*
WASHINGTON. . . . . *Western Hemlock*
WEST VIRGINIA . . . . *Sugar Maple*
WISCONSIN . . . . *Sugar Maple*
WYOMING. . . . . *Cottonwood*

The eyes of the world are upon you. The hopes and prayers of liberty-loving people everywhere march with you.

DWIGHT D. EISENHOWER

Here Rests in
  Honored Glory
An American Soldier
  Known But to God

THE TOMB OF THE
UNKNOWN SOLDIER

You can't appreciate home till you've left it, money till it's spent, your wife till she's joined a woman's club, nor Old Glory till you see it hanging on a broomstick on the shanty of a consul in a foreign town.

O. HENRY

The difficult we do immediately. The impossible takes a little longer.

SLOGAN OF U. S. ARMY AIR FORCES

Don't give up the ship!

JAMES LAWRENCE

Old soldiers never die; they just fade away.

DOUGLAS MACARTHUR

By the rude bridge that arched the flood,
    Their flag to April's breeze unfurled,
Here once the embattled farmers stood,
    And fired the shot heard round the world.

RALPH WALDO EMERSON

I only regret that I have but one life to lose for my country.

NATHAN HALE

Listen, my children, and you shall hear
Of the midnight ride of Paul Revere,
On the eighteenth of April, in Seventy-five;
Hardly a man is now alive
Who remembers that famous day and year.

HENRY WADSWORTH LONGFELLOW

Let me assert my firm belief that the only thing
we have to fear is fear itself.

FRANKLIN D. ROOSEVELT

Yankee Baked Beans

As John C. Bossidy said, *"And this is good old Boston. The home of the bean and the cod!"* A trip to Boston should include a stop for a meal featuring genuine baked beans. This recipe not only has the traditional molasses but a special dash of Worcestershire sauce as well.

½ POUND BACON

2 POUNDS CANNED BAKED BEANS

½ CUP CHOPPED ONION

¼ CUP HICKORY BARBECUE SAUCE

⅓ CUP CHILI SAUCE

3 TABLESPOONS DIJON MUSTARD

2 TABLESPOONS MOLASSES

1 TABLESPOON WORCESTERSHIRE

★ Preheat oven to 350°F. Butter a 1½-quart baking dish.

★ Cut the bacon into 1-inch pieces, then cook in a skillet over medium heat until crisp, turning once. Drain.

★ In a bowl, stir the undrained beans with the bacon and remaining ingredients.

★ Spoon into the prepared baking dish and bake 30 minutes, until bubbly.

MAKES 6 SERVINGS

Think of your forefathers and of your posterity.

JOHN QUINCY ADAMS

But at this point the immigrants' only concern was to get off Ellis Island. All of them looked in relief for the door that was marked "Push to New York." And they pushed. Now, after another ferry ride, they set foot on the earth of the land that was paved with gold.

ALISTAIR COOKE

There were human beings aboard the Mayflower,
Not merely ancestors.

STEPHEN VINCENT BENÉT

Mr. Kaplan sighed, straightened the envelope, smiled proudly at Mr. Parkhill, and read.
  "Dear Titcher—In Fabrary, ve got Judge Vashington's boitday, a fine holiday. Also Abram Lincohen's. In May ve got Memorable Day, for dad soldiers. In July comms, netcheral, Fort July. Also ve have Labor Day, Denksgivink, for de Peelgrims, an' for de feenish fromm de Voild Var, Armistress Day."

LEONARD Q. ROSS

Give me your tired, your poor,
Your huddled masses yearning to breathe free,
The wretched refuse of your teeming shore,
Send these, the homeless, tempest-tossed, to me:
I lift my lamp beside the golden door.

EMMA LAZARUS, THE STATUE OF LIBERTY

A *Nation of Immigrants.*

JOHN F. KENNEDY

I pledge allegiance to the flag of the United
States of America and to the republic for which it
stands, one nation, under God, indivisible, with
liberty and justice for all.

FRANCIS BELLAMY,
THE PLEDGE OF ALLEGIANCE TO THE FLAG

So at last I was going to America! Really, really,
going, at last! The boundaries burst. The arch of
heaven soared. A million suns shone out for every
star. The winds rushed in from outer space,
roaring in my ears, "America! America!"

MARY ANTIN

45

MEMORIAL DAY GREETINGS

LIBERTY FOR EVER

New York Egg Cream

A*nyone who grew up in New York City, from the Bronx to Brooklyn, claims that his or her corner candy store or soda fountain made the best egg creams. Containing neither egg nor cream, this chocolaty soda gets its name from the white foam on top that resembles whipped egg whites.*

1 CUP COLD MILK CHILLED SELTZER	⅓ CUP CHOCOLATE SYRUP

★ Pour the milk into a tall chilled glass.
★ Holding the seltzer bottle about 12 inches above the glass, slowly pour in the seltzer until the glass is three-fourths full and a high foam appears on the top.
★ Pour in the syrup, all at once.
★ Stir the egg cream quickly with a long-handled spoon, being careful to keep the foam.
★ Finish filling up the glass with the seltzer.

MAKES 1 EGG CREAM

47

Thanksgiving Day . . . the one day that is
purely American.

O. HENRY

The test of our progress is not whether we add
more to the abundance of those who have much;
it is whether we provide enough for those who
have too little.

FRANKLIN D. ROOSEVELT

And let these altars, wreathed with flowers
And piled with fruits, awake again
Thanksgivings for the golden hours,
The early and the latter rain!

JOHN GREENLEAF WHITTIER

Heap high the board with plenteous cheer, and
gather to the feast,
And toast the sturdy Pilgrim band whose
courage never ceased.
Give praise to that All-Gracious One by whom
their steps were led,
And thanks unto the harvest's Lord who sends
our "daily bread."

ALICE WILLIAMS BROTHERTON

Instead of comparing our lot with that of those who are more fortunate than we are, we should compare it with the lot of the great majority of our fellow men. It then appears that we are among the privileged.

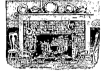

HELEN KELLER

 He'll labour night and day
To be a pilgrim.
JOHN BUNYAN

I wish the bald eagle had not been chosen as the representative of our country. . . . The turkey is a much more respectable bird, and withal a true original native of America.

BENJAMIN FRANKLIN

Afterwards the Lord sent them such seasonable showers, with fair, warm weather in between, that their harvest was a bountiful one. For this mercy they also set aside a day of thanksgiving as soon as it was convenient to do so.

GOVERNOR BRADFORD

FOURTH OF JULY GREETINGS

THOMAS JEFFERSON HANDING THE DECLARATION OF INDEPENDENCE TO "UNCLE SAM"

Summer Picnic Pickles

"He looks as if he had been weaned on a pickle." This line by Alice Roosevelt Longworth would never apply to anyone tasting these pickles, which are just sweet enough to make you smile.

12 KIRBY CUCUMBERS
2 CUPS PEARL ONIONS
½ CUP SALT
2 CUPS CIDER VINEGAR
½ CUP SUGAR
2 TEASPOONS CELERY SEEDS

2 TEASPOONS MUSTARD SEEDS
2 TEASPOONS PICKLING SPICE
2 TEASPOONS BLACK PEPPER
1 TEASPOON GINGER
1 TEASPOON TURMERIC

★ Slice the cucumbers and onions.
★ In a bowl, toss the cucumbers and onions with the salt, cover with cold water, and let stand 2 hours. Drain.
★ Place them in a saucepan and stir in the remaining ingredients.
★ Bring to a boil over medium-high heat, boil 1 minute, then remove and cool.
★ Spoon into jars and refrigerate. Enjoy all summer long!

MAKES 4 PINTS PICKLES

The country is the real thing, the substantial thing, the eternal thing; it is the thing to watch over, and care for, and be loyal to.

MARK TWAIN

THE HISTORY OF THE U.S.

In fourteen hundred ninety-two, Columbus sailed
    the ocean blue
And found this land, land of the Free, beloved by
    you, beloved by me.

★

And in the year sixteen and seven, good Captain
    Smith thought he'd reach Heav'n,
And then he founded Jamestown City, alas, 'tis
    gone, oh, what a pity.

★

'Twas in September sixteen nine, with ship, Half
    Moon, a real Dutch sign,
That Henry Hudson found the stream, the
    Hudson River of our dream.

★

In sixteen twenty pilgrims saw our land that had
    no unjust law.
Their children here in this day, proud citizens of
    U.S.A.

In sixteen hundred eighty-three, good William
      Penn stood 'neath a tree
And swore that unto his life's end he would be
      the Indian's friend.

In seventeen hundred seventy-five good Paul
      Revere was then alive;
He rode like wild throughout the night, and called
      the Minute Men to fight.

Year seventeen hundred seventy-six, July the
      fourth, this date please fix
Within your minds, my children dear, for that
      was Independence Year.

In that same year, on a bitter night at Trenton
      was an awful fight,
But by our brave George Washington the battle
      was at last well won.

Two other dates in your mind fix—Franklin born
      in seventeen six,
And Washington first said "Boo-Hoo" in
      seventeen hundred thirty-two.

In seventeen hundred seventy-nine, Paul Jones,
      who was a captain fine,
Gained our first naval victory fighting on the big,
      wide sea.

And in the year eighteen and four, Lewis and
      Clark both went before,

53

And blazed for us the Oregon trail where men go
  now in ease by rail.

★

In eighteen hundred and thirteen on great Lake
  Erie could be seen
Our Perry fight the Union Jack and drive it from
  our shores far back.

★

In eighteen hundred and sixty-one an awful war
  was then begun
Between the brothers of our land, who now
  together firmly stand.

★

In eighteen hundred sixty-three each slave was
  told that he was free
By Lincoln with whom few compare in being kind
  and just and fair.

★

In eighteen hundred eighty-one at Panama there
  was begun
By good De Lesseps, wise and great, the big
  canal, now our ships' gate.

★

At San Juan, eighteen ninety-eight, our brave
  Rough Riders lay in wait,
And on the land brought victory, while Dewey
  won it on the sea.

★

In nineteen hundred and fifteen was shown a
  panoramic screen
At San Francisco's wondrous fair; all people
  were invited there.

★

*But cruel war in that same year kept strangers
    from our land o' cheer,
And nineteen seventeen brought here the war
    that filled our hearts with fear.*

★

*Thank God in nineteen eighteen Peace on the
    earth again was seen,
And we are praying that she'll stay forever in our
    U.S.A.*

WINIFRED SACKVILLE STONER

Where liberty dwells there is my country.

THOMAS JEFFERSON

To waste, to destroy, our natural resources will
result in undermining in the days of our children
the very prosperity which we ought by right to
hand down to them amplified.

THEODORE ROOSEVELT

In the final analysis, our most basic common
link is that we all inhabit this small planet. We
all breathe the same air. We all cherish our
children's future. And we are all mortal.

JOHN F. KENNEDY

★ ★ ★ ★ ★ ★ ★ ★

I must study politics and war, that my sons
may have liberty to study mathematics and
philosophy, geography, natural history and naval
architecture, navigation, commerce, and
agriculture, in order to give their children a right
to study painting, poetry, music, architecture,
statuary, tapestry, and porcelain.

JOHN ADAMS

The world
is my country,
all mankind are
my brethren, and to
do good is my
religion.

THOMAS PAINE

We look forward to a world founded upon four
essential human freedoms. The first is freedom of
speech and expression—everywhere in the world.
The second is freedom of every person to worship
God in his own way—everywhere in the world.
The third is freedom from want . . . everywhere in
the world. The fourth is freedom from fear . . .
anywhere in the world.

FRANKLIN D. ROOSEVELT

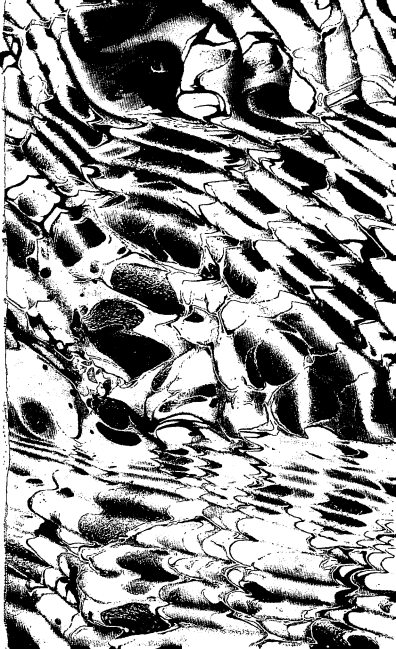

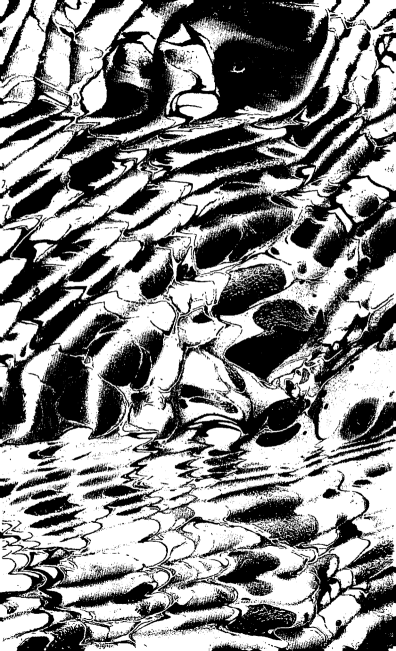